NOT
WITHOUT
OUR
LAUGHTER

POEMS OF HUMOR, JOY & SEXUALITY

NOT WITHOUT OUR LAUGHTER

POEMS OF HUMOR, JOY & SEXUALITY

BLACK LADIES BRUNCH COLLECTIVE

Printed in Honesdale, PA by Spencer Printing.o

Layout and cover design by Ian Anderson.

Published and distributed by
Mason Jar Press
Baltimore, MD 21218

Learn more about Mason Jar Press at
masonjarpress.xyz.

NOT WITHOUT...

...OUR MOODS AND FOODS

...OUR MISBEHAVIOR?

...OUR GOOD HOUSEKEEPING?

...OUR LISTS AND LITANIES

...OUR BODY POLITICS

...OUR TECHNOLOGY

...OUR DIVINE CHORDS

THE BLACK LADIES BRUNCH COLLECTIVE IS:

SAIDA AGOSTINI
ANYA CREIGHTNEY
TERI ELLEN CROSS DAVIS
CELESTE DOAKS
TAFISHA EDWARDS
KATY RICHEY

EDITOR'S NOTE

In May 2014, a group of black women gathered over brunch to commune with one another and talk poetry. Eventually this group developed into the Black Ladies Brunch Collective (BLBC) which today includes Saida Agostini, Anya Creightney, Teri Ellen Cross Davis, celeste doaks, Tafisha Edwards and Katy Richey. As a group identity began to grow, we hoped to do something more impactful in the world at large. That significance was in proposing (and being accepted) for a group reading in the Spring 2016 Split This Rock poetry festival. Our reading entitled "Not Without Laughter," was based on the title and ideology of a Langston Hughes novel. The funny and provocative reading was such a hit that audience members asked if we would be taking our "show" on the road, and did we have books for sale? We weren't, and didn't, as of yet, but the wheels began to turn. We met Ian and Michael at Mason Jar Press andv the rest is history. As the saying goes, if you build it...

BLBC hails from Africa, Ireland, Guyana, Native America, Jamaica, Denmark, Baltimore, Virginia, Silver Spring, DC, and many other locales. We identify as straight, gay, bisexual, black, biracial, Caribbean, Midwestern, East Coast, West Coast, and everything in between. In my opinion, "We come in too many flavors for one fucking spoon," as poet, playwright and memoirist Staceyann Chin says in her poem "Womanist or Feminist." We laugh, fight and love hard—both in and out of our collective. That's who we are as black female poets.

On the page, each of us brings our own unique, individual perspective to this collection. Some topics we will explore here include, but are not limited to, romantic and familial relationships, mental stability and self-care, sex and sexuality, gender biases, and domestic responsibilities. Read, for instance, Teri's misadventure with Frank the roach, which reverberates off Lucille Clifton's "cruelty. don't talk to me about cruelty or what I am capable of." Check out Anya's "Leaving the House," which gives us the bold swagger we need to go into the world. Cackle at a *hoo ha* in Tafisha's "Top Billing," as she talks about it like it's a rock star (and maybe it is). Be astounded at spectacular strap-ons or quietly reminded how precious Grandmommas are in Saida's poems. Marvel at how unity can be found through a green vegetable or how to celebrate the successes and struggles of mental illness in Katy Richey's poems. Or take an imaginary ride on the back of a Harley with me, destination unknown. *Not Without Our Laughter: Poems of Humor, Joy and Sexuality* is a book that considers the real and the fictional, tapping into black female legacies as historical as Sojourner Truth and as contemporary as Olivia Pope.

Black women's voices have been historically and tragically marginalized, generalized, ignored, overlooked, and devalued. BLBC aims to lift up, promote and inspire the voices of black women. Understandably, the voices of black males have been highlighted due to the scourge of police brutality, but the chorus of resistance must be "not without our laughter." Not without the voices of black women, and not without our laughter, our joy, our desire. This collection is one remedy. The previous year has been fraught. From an attack on young black teens at a Texas pool party, to Rachel Dolezal's "passing blackness," to the massacre of nine churchgoers in Charleston, and culminating in a presidential election the results of which BLBC laments daily—disheartening news seems ever-present. But African Americans have always battled sorrow with laughter. As Hughes so eloquently states in his poem "The Jester": "In one hand / I hold tragedy / And in the other / Comedy—." Comic resistance has always been a deeply rooted African American tradition.

Without laughter, how would we progress? Historically, African Americans have not waited for the transformation of society in order to laugh. Our humor has always been a salve for survival in the worst of times. As Langston Hughes says in his first novel, many "poverty-stricken Negroes ... lived so long ... because to them, no matter how hard life might be, it was not without laughter." Laughter is a piece of that better world that we envision for the future. And the laughter of black people, more specifically black women—earthy, stinging at times, warmly embracing at others—is all the more so.

The six female poets of BLBC offer their humorous and joyful work in Not Without Our Laughter as an attempt towards healing. As we Americans work through tough issues, what offers light in our darkest hours? What poetic words of levity provide inspiration? *Not Without Our Laughter* is our contribution of small triumphs, and sometimes failures, during these troubled times. It is our solace through humor. This book is our invitation to temporary shelter from the storm, an invitation we as black women extend to any and all readers, no matter their gender, sexual orientation, race, or ethnicity. We welcome whomever can tap into our poems for inspiration in their own struggles towards light, harmony, togetherness, joy.

When I begin to think about the totality of this collection and how it began, I get emotional. I feel overjoyed and grateful that six women gathering to commune over omelets and mimosas can produce a moving, delightful, and diverse anthology of poems. I am blessed and elated to edit and contribute to *Not Without Our Laughter*. BLBC thinks of this collection the way audre lorde ends her poem "Coal": "I am black because I come from the earth's inside / take my word for jewel in your open light." Therefore dear reader, we hope our poems generate some laughs, a few warm smiles, and maybe a tear or two. We hope to keep you sane in the struggle, and ultimately remind you of what it is we struggle for.

—CELESTE DOAKS

OUR
MOODS AND FOODS

LEAVING THE HOUSE
Anya Creightney

I am going out in the world resolved to act boogaloo and bug-eyed, to say something real nasty in 7/11 or on the subway. Maybe Simone White is right, I got a chicken wing twitch of the right arm, which is to say, I'm either gonna out order the darkest motherfucker in the rib joint or write a postcard in the fancy part of town, knocking real neighbor-like on some ornate door asking for postage. And I'm no star but I am gonna spend serious money on skincare at Barneys. During checkout, I'll use nothing but outdated slang. Scratch. Scrilla. Anna. Chedda. Fetta. Cheese. Or how about Little Tokyo? I'm gonna order mullato right off the menu easy as pie. Self-made, I'm gonna Archie Bunker his armchair at the National Museum of American History. Scatterbrained, I'm gonna smear my fingerprints all over the damn thing. And when it's all over and provocation comes I can say I did it. I mean it.

DEPRESSION INSISTS WE STAY IN

Katy Richey
after Leaving the House

There's not a single thing in your closet
that should be worn after 1997.
You do look fat in those pants,
probably gained twenty pounds
in the last thirty minutes. There's no parking
within ten blocks of the party.
All the people you hate are already there.
They're miserable too, but tonight
you won't be able to tell. They'll have
green string tied around their middle fingers
and you're supposed to know why.
There will be twenty-two words spoken
you don't know the meaning of.
You will end all your sentences with prepositions.
People will notice. People will laugh
when others mention Gary Johnson.
You never Googled Aleppo. You don't know
what it is either. All your "friends" will ask
if you're okay, remark that you're always
so down-to-earth. This will remind you
the entire world lies. You'll think about
Lance Armstrong and Milli Vinilli
and your best friend who made out
with your very first boyfriend
while you were home with strep. You slept
with his letter jacket, had to wash
the snot/drool/tear stains in the sink.
You loved John Hughes movies.
If you stay, you can watch The Breakfast Club

for the 57th time. Pinkie swear you won't think
about self-harm. Swear you won't imagine
all the ways this could end.
Think of the relationships you neglect
by leaving—the inanimate objects to be moved
and then replaced right back
where they were—the two Oreo cookies
left in the package to reassure
you didn't eat them all at once.
Think about the floor in the bathroom,
how much more sense things make lying
with your bare back on the tile. This is you.
You are the plate and the half-eaten sandwich.
You're the pile of laundry. Don't forget how
Barney-the-purple-dinosaur-meaningless
it is out there. This stain on the carpet is you.
These unread books—you. Don't forget you.

ACCEPTING PEAS—OR THE THINGS YOU CANNOT CHANGE

Katy Richey

I love the smallness
of you, how you fight
the fork, your belly
glass and mold
like the body
of a neglected
aquarium.
I long to push you,
hear the deafening
scrape of your
defiance.
When you and I
become one, our blood
merges, our mucus
tangles, my lips
purse in reverie.

THAT TIME I PUT LIVER IN MY PANTIES

Teri Ellen Cross Davis

My mother knew my sister and I hated liver
still, she tried to feed her children the cheap,
vitamin-rich organ meat. She'd smother
its death smell in a cast-iron skillet,
surround it with a waste of heavenly
bacon, onions, anything to make it palatable
to the picky birds that were her daughters.
After our noses turned up, she'd ask
Did you cook it? Then she'd deliver
the hard line—Y'all going to eat what I cook.
But liver was a deal-breaker.
(Followed closely by okra's mucus
and the crimson torture of beets.)
Dinner became a dance of forks:
a little hide and seek under bread crusts,
some twirling in mashed potatoes,
some accidentally scraped under
the plate's rim, only a few bites making it past
our gratuitous gag reflexes. Until one fortunate
skate of tine found liver chunks delivered
neatly into my lap and my hands swiftly
squirreled those putrid squares into my panties.
The math of unlimited bathroom breaks quickly
added another escape route for the fetid meat;
but smart parents realized after three
allowed trips to the bathroom, a third of liver
was still left to "eat." So it was a garbled I'm finished
through a mouthful, a surreptitious sprint
through the kitchen-adjacent garage door,

and the gray meat was neatly deposited into the first
empty container I could find—a blue Solo cup
in the window sill. So days later when the liver
had grown friends of the squirming, sightless
white kind, my father asked, What that's smell?
Under the feigned innocence, I rejoiced.
A clean getaway never smelled so foul.

OUR
MISBEHAVIOR?

HUSBANDS

Tafisha Edwards

What if the woman whose husband I want to fuck cuts my throat and glitter rushes out over her hands, a sea of shine, and what if the husband I want to fuck stands next

to the woman who holds the knife covered in glitter, and says nothing about the soft phepphepphep that is miniscule pieces of plastic, trillions of pieces of plastic,

bounding out of my cut carotid artery, like children loose after eight hours of cramming their torsos under desks at the threat of a bomb, or a gun, or The Bomb, not high on

sugarsaltsun, but on amphetamines and the elasticity of their own legs? What if the husband of the woman who washes the glitter off of her hands only touched

me once? And it wasn't a touch, it was a hug? And it didn't really last that long, because the husband in question is not a wolf, and he loves the woman he calls his wife,

and I need him to be a good man, and he needs to be a good man too because we fucked up by talking about God, and now there is a guilt that makes it fun, except

he really does believe in God and really wants to lick every molar in the roller rink of my mouth. What if they bury me under their jungle gym of a Birch tree, what if

the slitting of my throat is a team building exercise and when someone that could only be him taps my shoulder to hide the oncoming edge of shine I shiver like light volleying

off a disco ball, and yes, that felt a bit random, but let's run with it because that is what wanting a married man is: one afterschoolsugarrushdash. What if I am trouble?

I mean what if I am bad news? And the wanting of a married man is a vitamin deficiency I have no interest in curing?

ADVENTURES OF THE THIRD LIMB

Saida Agostini

I want to name our cock chocolate thunder, tammy thinks
I have lost my mind. I see our cock as a blaxsploitation heroine
resplendent in the finest of neon spandex, draped in golden chains
and a velvet cape, stiff in resolution to kick any jive turkey punk
muthafucka ass into submission.

our cock has framed pictures of prince on the wall, and listens
to deon estus to show her sensitive side.

she is fluent in seven languages, drinks dos equis, can paint, sing gospel,
praise dance and is head usher at the church of dynamic discipleship.
our cock is the renaissance dick, and if you are looking at her sideways:
bitch, what has your cock done for you lately?

our cock doesn't hide when company comes, stalks out butt-naked
in sequined pumps, shining with lube, sits spread eagled on
the dinner table and says embarrassing shit about things she
would do to kerry washington.

and when everyone else leaves, and only the three of us are left,
all limbs and laughter, she pulls me and tammy closer, our pussies climbing
up her veined girth.

this is how we fit together—loud, tight and eager, our wails her
composition, agitated aching notes—accesso and broken
chord. in the studio later with smokey, outfitted in a double breasted
stacey adams suit, matching gators, pinky ring and straw panama hat, she'll share a blunt,
and then play cruisin while talking shit about how hard we came, and the scent of wet
—but in that moment,   oh!   my love!

A HARLEY DREAM

celeste doaks

he is hot fudge topping
dripping over shiny silver piping
of the Harley
tattoos decorate bulky cocoa arms
like freckles on a map that
make me want to sail the world
my eyes drive north to an avocado
colored bandana that probably covers
a slick bald head shining
like daddy's Sunday shoes
juicy lips peek out
from underneath a broom-like moustache
filled with black and grey rattlesnakes,
the ones who strike silently,
prey on a girl like me

your bike careens down the highway
which becomes a long strip
of salty bacon that stretches on
no end in sight
past Stella's skyline Café
where other Daytona bikers convene
attached to stringy haired wives
with tugboats and Dos Equis Beer bottles
inked on breasts or ankles
i wonder would you queen me
Your Cinderella
rescue me from a life of tortuous toil
we could traverse down 95

stopping along at Scottsmoor
rest at a seedy motel
where a blazing neon orange sign
would wink at us
our room would be filled with pot smoke,
strewn Bacardi bottles
and various leather sex contraptions
i would die my afro violet
get everything below the navel pierced
only call my parents at rest stops
where the bathrooms reeked of piss
left longer than the scribbled in 'call me' numbers

We would continue this for days
eventually reaching Miami's nape
when i would notice my monthly
moon marker missing
you'd grumble grizzly objections
but deep down i'd know
we'd just turn right back around
repeating our reckless rode-bound wanderlust
i'd try to quit the cancer sticks, liquor,
appetite for threesomes
and settle into the newness of my belly full
with a carbon copy you

i awake from this dream rocking, turning
into the thin veined dirt road

of my temporary new home thinking
what if i'd sprung from the car
mounted myself behind you
pressed my breasts to your back
the gas fumes tickling my nose hairs
the vibration of the machine pleading
who would care as long as
those yellow dashes would skip
down the road dotting and dashing
like Morse code forever

KAMAL & BEEBEE

Anya Creightney
after A Harley Dream &
after Baby What That Mouth Do

desire is a wild
boundary like a ludicrous
or endangered animal
(platypus or kookaburra)

& all words sound
sexual, especially "calvados"
with its bestial root center,
or "mammal" with its mouth
full of meat

so it's not a tad surprising
that a woman called Beebee
loves someone named Kamal
each on all fours
mooing rhythmically,
mooing percussively,
into the air

together their ravenous
laughter is winding smilax

& isn't it funny to feel
so vulnerable to wild
undressing, when
vulnerability is partly the point

the paradox,
an unforgettable addition like
a blade of light in what
was once a dark house

& soon Beebee will know if
Kamal's hip sings as a violin
or piccolo.

HARRIET TUBMAN IS A LESBIAN

Saida Agostini

jabari says fuck that, harriet wasn't trying turn the underground into henrietta's. but shit, I need a hero, a full on black queer woman setting fire to slave ships, cursing out white motherfuckers and going home to love on phyllis hyman's fine-assed great great granny. I want a history where harriet and sojourner get together and make cataclysmic, head banging good god kind of love while luther serenades them, with skin so shining it looks like he just swam all up in johnson and johnson's to get there. I want him singing to them, his sequined blazer the north star they follow hand in hand under the cover of knotted trees and vines rising up to hide them. the glow of lightning bugs, grasshoppers humming as luther executes a smooth two step to wait for love—prince behind him humping the stage. and that moment when sojourner bends down, cups her hands, dips them into a running creek and says, c'mon harriet, drink, watches the soft pulse and bend of her woman's neck as she feeds sweet water from her palm—and she thinks someday I'll make me a poem about how I love her. I think that night would be the first time they must have found the salt to kiss, during intermission while luther reapplies his eyeliner, and prince takes over the mic crooning baby baby baby what's it going to be tonight, sojourner and harriet latching on to each other's bodies, sucking nipples like they deliver wine, hollering a blue joyful streak in answer to prince over and over again.

KNOWLEDGE OF THE BROWN BODY

Teri Ellen Cross Davis
after harriet tubman is a lesbian

If Harriet Tubman had been a lesbian
I would know the brown body had been
valued outside of chattel, to the point of risk.
I would know an ebony nipple spoke its hushed
volumes from inside another sweet brown mouth
eager to know its secrets. I would know a brown
belly had been showered with a free tongue's pulsing
intention. I would know the brown hips of a woman
were stolen back for freedom's sake. I would know
that brown thighs' thunder was enough to make a woman walk
into the abyss of the deep South and come out clapping,
on fire with black love. I would know that this body I own,
had once been coveted for its sake and its sake alone.
How sacred I could hold that knowledge, I could palm it,
my fingers deep inside the agent that helped break
the back of the Confederacy.

OUR
GOOD
HOUSEKEEPING?

SIR RODERICK

Tafisha Edwards

It just never occurred to you that something sentient
would emerge from the hole beneath the radiator in the hole
that is your apartment so you do the thing where you yelp
because something is alive in your house besides you,
(narcissistic much?) and this something has a tiny parasympathetic

nervous system and some sort of cognitive ability (the expanding hole
in the rice cake bag sure wasn't made by you) and so killing
your new roommate is becoming an increasingly unattractive option
—especially when you start thinking about Sir Roderick's
(isn't that a fun name?) fifteen infant blind mice and how it would
devastate the brood (and the larger mouse community) if you killed

the head of their household (isn't that technically you though?)
and now you have the blood of imaginary blind caretaker-less baby
mice on your hands, congratu-fucking-lations. Your guilt won't allow
you to pour boiling water or glue or acetone or anything containing
high fructose corn syrup down the hole where the mouse and its brood

of blind children squeak, or call maintenance even though you lie
to everyone at the Friday team meeting and say you did, and in return
your tenant agrees to limit striving for basic sustenance between the hours
of 11 p.m. to 5 a.m. Since you should be asleep at that time anyway
you call it a deal and shake out your blankets night in case he reneges.

FRANK

Teri Ellen Cross Davis

Roaches know they are supposed to scurry,
inheriting genetic knowledge of light
as enemy, its brightness followed swiftly
by the final darkness of a shoe. So when we flicked
the kitchen switch of our first apartment,
we became used to the brown scatter, segmented legs
fleeing, sounding like pennies shifting in a tin pan.
Imagine our surprise to see one left behind.
His back, twice the height of his fleet brethren.
It's humped, lopsided nature prohibiting a fast
getaway. We guessed his abnormality the result
of an exterminator gel meant to cause
sterilization in the next roach generation,
at least that's what the landlord told us,
the young couple taking the cheapest apartment
next to the trash chute. We believed him. We stayed.
But roaches are built for the fast getaway,
six legs attached to a thorax, cursorial appendages
that if lost or smashed, grow back. But his uneven
load kept him going in circles and circles.
So we had time, between retrieving a hard-heeled boot,
to laugh until bent over with tears, eventually creating
a narrative, giving him a name worthy of a story,
worthy of his ignominious departure from this life.

THE PERFECT SIGN, OR TOO MUCH WINE, NOT ENOUGH GRATIN

celeste doaks

Honestly, I was nervous because we never had our tarot cards read together
or our palm lines read by some woman covered in turquoise,
but the symbols we did have were nebulous. Co-habitation felt
like a boxing match—we each bit down hard on our mouth guards,
laced up our boots, and got ready to spar. You loved the silverware ends up,
the forks and knives threatening to send my delicate hands to the ER.
I preferred them down just like I did the toilet tissue roll. Am I the only one
who thinks the squares should be pulled down when you're perched
on the commode? Anyways, you enjoy the apartment blinds pulled up,
obviously adore the neighbors getting a full view of our naked bodies
during lovemaking. And I love the slats closed, so no one can spot
my mis-matched panties and bra as I race for my cup of morning joe.

But this holiday, we promised, would be perfect. We'd already
drank one bottle of Pinot, a celebratory toast for ducking our families
and staying home solo to cook. And I assumed the smashed grapes
rolling around in our blood would help my fiancé cut the potatoes, drown them
in olive oil and spices, and bake them to a brown better than a Kardashian's next
tanning session. As for my own dinner contribution, it was already done:
stuffed salmon, steaming and arranged on the plate polite as a child
sitting on a church pew. After the spuds were dressed and baking,
we opened the second bottle. A corner-store Merlot inspired some kissing,
caressing of thighs and navels as sweaters and corduroys fell to the floor.
And just before we got to what my auntie calls "the meat of the sandwich,"
we heard a pop, then an explosion, or maybe a collision of sorts. Glass smashing
into metal and the slow hissss of oil burning. And no, we never flipped
The Lovers card or intercepted a Hail Mary in the 4th quarter,
but our first turkey day was a delightful disaster. A wonderful failure.
And as we stood, half-dressed in front of the oven door, the cookware severed
into pieces, the remnants of our gratin sliding down the oven wall,
we took this as omen. Maybe these greasy potatoes infused with glass
were the cowrie shells. Maybe this was all we needed.

OUR
LISTS AND LITANIES

13 REASONS WHY I LOVE LONG JOHN BOTTOMS

celeste doaks
dedicated to Kelle Groom

Long john bottoms offer the option to go Commando!
They make me feel like Irene Cara from Fame.
They are a warm hug before leaving for school
or work, and since I'm neurotic about being
appropriately dressed for functions, they are easily
an extra outfit option.

When my flannel pajamas aren't clean,
I do occasionally sleep in them.
My blue jeans don't rub in the middle
when I wear my long john bottoms.

All ladies know these things prevent
unworthy men from getting to the goods
too quickly. My long john bottoms,
made by Cuddl Duds, have a silk finish
that helps me slide up and down
hardwood floors with ease—
like a seven-year-old whose parents
aren't home.

And this pseudo-child loves
the quiet swisssh sound they make
when my thighs kiss in between.
Plus, they make my butt look bigger;
and who couldn't use some help
in that department? With long john
bottoms on, my sometimes unshaven legs
are an even bigger secret to the world.

These winter saviors come in black,
white, or nude; and I simply love
being able to say, "I have on nude pants."
But mostly, long john bottoms remind me
of my ex and our visit across the pond;
us loving in a Kensington hotel room
where he couldn't wait
to pull them off.

THERAPY

Katy Richey

Write a letter to your mother, but don't send it
Write a letter to your uncle, lover, abuser
Write a letter to yourself,
Title it: Dear, Just Need to Smile More
Take your medication
Don't send anything
Make a plan
Make a collage,
Title it: Living Things
Find a therapist
Find a calling
Find god
Get an exorcism
Consult a healer
Get a dog
Get a grip
Get electric shock
Believe you can heal
Take your meds
Talk to your doctor,
You can't be helped if you don't talk
Smile more
Do yoga
Do yoga while burning incense
Burn your yoga mat
Burn all the letters
Make amends
Make a list
Make it all up

STEPS TO HEALING

Saida Agostini
after Therapy

1. listen to luther non stop

2. wear low cut shirts

3. quit your job by staging a praise dance version of Beyonce's Freedom in front of your racist ass boss. get the cashier at seven eleven to do kendrick lamar's verse.

4. call your granny, cry

5. cry again with your Daddy

6. end the call when he asks about your 401k

7. think about the positives about the Trump administration—namely Pence's hair, how does a white man get his hair so on fleek? Does he use blue magic? Does he have a black barber? Is his name Lamont? is Lamont a Republican? Did Lamont give Pence a du rag? Does Pence wear the du rag during Black History month?

8. call your granny again, discuss Pence's hair, compare it with Bernie's at the DNC. Listen to her hushed whispers in the bathroom when she shares that Bernie could get it.

9. weep again in your white therapist's office

10. listen as your white therapist says, I don't really think trump will round up all black lgbtq people

11. wonder how she quantifies all. would all include everybody except Lamont? Pence's lover? Who are the exclusions?

12. realize you are weary of white disbelief.

13. look at her face while you are crying. see her eyes water. they are probably allergies. she tells you she is probably safe.

14. read of the 8 trans people who have committed suicide since the elections.

15. think of pence again and all the black and queer blood on his hands. Trump's silly wig and the million dollars he has invested in the pipeline.

16. read Macbeth. imagine trump in tights and a cockpiece. sage your eyes.

17. research visas to Guyana. think about whether or not the closet could look good on you. Realize the only gay woman you know of in Guyana is a lady boxer. Research on facebook for the said lady boxer for 45 minutes until you realize that "lady boxer" is probably not her name. Her name is most likely "Eunice" or "Marjorie"

18. text back and forth with Blair about countries to move to. think of how blackness is a gamble wherever
you go.

19. when you think of home, you think of granny, a 90 year old woman, a living altar rooted here.

20. ask your heart if it can flee.

21. listen to the answer

11 THINGS I'VE LEARNED AT PINCH'S TRIVIA NIGHT

celeste doaks

1. Don't assume your husband knows all the answers, especially when it comes to pop culture. His being an avid Cavs fan doesn't necessarily make him a sports guru.

2. Make sure to pee long before the 1st round starts because trying to clench and hold it all the way through the bonus questions is futile.

3. France is the country with the largest geographical surface area out of all the EU nations.

4. Recruit family members, work colleagues, people I met six minutes ago, ex-boyfriends (just kidding honey), vagabonds from the street—anyone who regards and retains minute details that I often find superfluous.

5. Imbibing lemon drop shots (that you won during round one) for a correct answer doesn't make my game stronger the same way an extra beer during pool seems to sink balls quicker.

6. Another word for the egg white is albumen. The albus is the Latin base that means white. Next time I'm in Starbucks I'll be sure to ask for an albumen and cheese sandwich and see if the cashier has any clue what I'm asking for.

7. Katy Perry has the most followers on Twitter even though I guessed Taylor Swift. I was wrong for thinking scandal draws in people like flies.

8. Nerdy looking kids win every time. Behind their glasses, polyester slacks, and laughs that sound like snorts lurk supernatural memory skills. I wonder if they drink blueberry smoothies and eat beet salads all day.

9. Although the host has said "no googling allowed" some people will still sneak a glance underneath the table.

10. How to control my face when the table next to me high fives and squeals after discovering they got the bonus round correct. This is an invaluable skill.

11. I should've known that Edgar Allen Poe was born in Boston, although he lived in Baltimore. I am a poet for God sakes.

SHIT AIN'T NEVER SIMPLE
Teri Ellen Cross Davis

I believe that what doesn't kill you had better make you stronger.

I believe that strength ain't necessarily seen from the outside.

I believe violence is rarely the answer but that some people deserve a good ass-whupping.

I believe there should be a Department for Peace.

I believe that no person has the power to break you, unless you give up that power.

I believe love is about knowing when to break down the barriers you put up

for the rest of the knuckleheaded hard-legs.

I believe that a lady should know how to curse properly.

I believe that a lady should know how to get into a car in a short skirt.

I believe in guys opening car doors.

I believe a woman should know how to drive stick.

I believe in nigga beaters.

I believe there is a difference between niggas and black folks.

I believe you should keep a little of that crazy nigga inside you for special occasions.

I believe in table manners.

I believe in dinner in front of the tv and by candlelight.

I believe in chopping wood for real fires.

I believe in axes over a gun any day.

I believe in getting dirt literally under your nails.

I believe that trying to figure out who you are is a worthy life ambition.

I believe one monkey don't stop no show.

I believe crying over a book means it was a good book.

I believe you mess with my kids, you mess with me.

I believe in waiting to the last minute.

I believe in the power of revision.

I believe that there will still be something left of me on the page before I die.

OUR
BODY POLITICS

TAKE OVER

Anya Creightney

Go on plastic body, make a spoon, make a spork. At 23 weeks a woman's womb is a grapefruit. At 6 weeks a pea. And radio is one gorgeous box. On call-ins you can speak to New York, Helsinki, Shanghai. It is your electronic friend. See? Go on plastic body, new raindrop. Go on. Right now there's a man alone in a room, his voice like a friend. I'm a cloud. I go anywhere I want, he says, feeling bold. The sky like crystalline jelly. So go on, liquid face, plastic body. In your hand an Easter basket is one long braid. Inside, colored eggs like Jordan almonds. Tinsel like sheared straw. Yes, go on, strange body, strange lightning. Go on dandelion spray. You can be anything you want.

DEFENDANT VS. HER REMAINING EGGS

Katy Richey

They're seated like justices, tapping their microphones,
raising their tiny gavels, setting them down again.

In the space set for the accused, I sometimes sit in spotlight,
other times a shameful darkness in a hat made for women fools.

They have their questions: How long do I plan denial? Have I considered
self sacrifice? What about that one who hummed a little while he slept?

They stir like molecules, nod their agreement or dissent—
When the door opens, it's the one on the end who must leave.

The others glance the space she leaves behind, some weep,
some make whispers, all turn their hollow eyes back to me.

WHAT IT TAKES TO BREATHE

Saida Agostini
~*for m.*

I have snored so loud I made friends weep for my next breath, swear
there is a whole carnival alive in my chest, aching beyond ribcage, to where my heart
lays smothered in veins, and fat—the swollen lungs seated, a fearful and
ready king above it all, gasping for a new swallow of breath to crown its life

imagine all this machinery just to breathe
the whole map of an exquisite monarchy drawn and refinished every time
my lungs expand.
⠀⠀⠀⠀—truly, there should be royal balls and prince singing adore each time I wake
everything is alive and green, the whole world thronging in ready with applause

I am foolish and tired, and cannot help but blush at the strangest things—
like the dawn of your eyes
greeting mine.

imagine all this machinery just to love

ARS POETICA WITH FEVER

Anya Creightney

after the snowstorm
I made myself ill
constructed sentences
like a charm bracelet

(a real humpty dumpty)

and when the telephone rang
I wore my big hair
like a hat

a huge hot hat

no that can't be right no

after the snowstorm
a fat truck drove around
the block like a saltlick

dogs walked themselves
home and our yard was dirty
meringue

(I got in bed with a bad case
of metaphor)

I drank fizzy drink and tolerated
my leaky face

I dreamt I fell over
board though a broad navy
man spotted me
thrashing in oversize
camouflage pajamas

(no dramatics I merely fell
for aquamarine)

when I woke syntax
was burning up its odd force
pure dynamite

when I woke light
went in my body my body
one atomic flower after another

ATOMIC SNOWSTORM

Tafisha Edwards
after Ars Poetic with Fever

after the snowstorm

(I got in bed with pajamas
a bad case
and when the home telephone rang
our yard was dirty
I drank fizzy drink tolerated
one flower after another

my leaky face man
spotted me
I wore my big hair
like camouflage
like a charm bracelet

I dreamt I fell over
board through a broad navy
(a real humpty dumpty)
dogs walked themselves
a fat truck drove around
the block like a saltlick

when I woke syntax
no that can't be right no

when I woke light
was burning up its odd force
went in my body my body
meringue
pure dynamite
a huge
hot hat
of metaphor)

I made myself ill

BABY, WHAT THAT MOUTH DO

Tafisha Edwards

Translation: "Can you please lick my vagina tonight?" which is another way
to say, "I hope you don't mind that I didn't shave because I didn't
want a razor that close to my clit," code for "I'm trying to rebel against
The Patriarchy and someone on Yahoo Answers told me this was a great
way to start," a euphemism for "This will determine if I need to break up
with you so licking my vagina is pretty monumental to the future of our relationship,"
implying deep thought about our relationship has occurred but does not mean
I don't like you tremendously, only that I have options, underscoring the fact
that I am twenty-four and unmarried, underscoring the fact I am not my mother
—I did something different, circling back to my family probably didn't think
different included Fluexotine, polyamory, and black feminist socio-economic
theory, but I know this is what they'll say: "She was always a strange one.
This is what happens when you send girls to school. This is American corruption
at its finest" which is just a Thing My Family Must Deal With. That thought provides
me with great joy in times of drought, wherein drought is an opaque way
of mentioning my not too long ago mental collapse—something that may or may
not still be in progress—although it should be noted that I did not die
Morbid thought, sure, but necessary, as it is the justification for this poem,
which was written in-spite and not because of a momentary lapse in productivity;
that last clause being an example of how a body can at times be regarded as a machine,
also an allusion to my distaste towards the ever earnest Protestant Work Ethic but,
in all fairness, may just be a manifestation of my innate laziness, which is not the
worst thing if you think about it, and while you think about it give me your hand,
touch my slippery slick, see your Darling Nikki's love unfurl, all this love, uncoiling
just for you.

MANIFESTO OF A BORN AGAIN INTERNAL ORGAN

Katy Richey

It's not that this is a repression,
being the vagina isn't as restrictive
as it might seem. I'm not unaware
of my obligations. I'm the muscle,
security, custodian of entrances and
exits. I don't feel suffocated, exactly,
but, sleeping naked on weekends
just isn't enough anymore. Everyone
says I should take a vacation, travel,
see Paris. I'd be happy just to smell
freshly fallen leaves in the backyard,
gaze my eye on the sun's red mouth
as it sets behind the neighbor's roof.

Don't misconstrue this statement
as discontent. See it more as an airing,
or disclosure of disenchantment.
It's not that I haven't had suitors.
Some gentleman, some scoundrel,
but all with a certain lure, an appeal
masking proclivities. I have felt
loved, even honored, but when I say
no more bartenders, I have to mean it
this time. I need to feel this merging
is more than an assembly of parts, that
however brief the suspension of disbelief,
afterwards, I take some of it with me.

I am still certain of many things, like
love and that menstrual pads shouldn't
also be underwear. Thongs are tortures
created by the devil. That hasn't changed.
But I'm beginning to recognize intention,
to see creativity in invention. I don't
have to participate to appreciate—pantyhose,
or the female condom, Twitter, or fantasy football.

It isn't that I'm unsatisfied, but I've heard
that some see heaven. All I've ever seen
is myself. I have seen my loveliness.
Even in darkness there's a shimmering,
phosphorescence in the water. I need to be more
than beautiful, more than an idol, adornment,
a served purpose. I want to hear my own name,
not the myriad of nicknames reflecting only
my sweetness, or bitterness, or cavernous.
V-A-G-I-N-A—I want to hear it with the same
favor one might say God or Madame President.
It isn't that I'm ungrateful, it's just I feel
something else coming.

TOP BILLING

Tafisha Edwards

Starring My Pussy as

Black peach Dancehall queen
Doom of Man™
Slip 'n' Slide command: "Don't touch that in front of people"
The dark & the tunnel & the creatureless lagoon
Blood pudding
Catfish lipped vortex of doom
"Get in free before 11" text
Area 52
  That impromptu party you threw
  at your parents house when you were 15
  that was totally worth the ass kicking
  they gifted you
Question: "What are you doing with your hand?"
Answer: "Touching"
My own Mound of Oshun

OUR
TECHNOLOGY

CATFISH: THE ORIGINAL

Saida Agostini

common sense should've told you that the night equaled trouble
after that cross-eyed-barely-average sister rolled up to you when
she promised poetic justice's janet jackson on blackplanet.
who knows why y'all kept going. maybe it was
the metronome of her ass swinging in those black tights,
or nasir laughing at you from the driver's seat, or the fact
that henrietta's was the right up the street, and when you get there,
there is some fine woman with an arc of ready hip to burrow into your side,
honey brown titties, and soft, wet lips that dare your ears to strain its belief

honestly, your roommate's rent money is burning a hole in your back pocket,
the thrum of liquor and ll cool j's bass line from doin' it has enchanted your hands.
and you aren't the first fool to get lost for a second in the flowering easy softness
of another woman. you found paradise in a cinnamon form and teeth tugging
on the back of your neck. you tell her I want you to have my baby and both laugh
with the desire of it, knowing wherever your bodies land—should they collide
in the stank-assed bathroom stall where no black woman would act like they fuck,
or fall like stars on the ground, cutting smooth and low, knees pressed up against titties
you have memorized (like the first hello)—it all means nothing without a name.
you aren't allowed precision upon first meeting, couch desires in mundane terms.
don't say, I want to leave something inside you that can't be forgotten. your fingers
weaved up inside like salmon swimming upstream through
a narrow pink canal into the uterus. say your fingers bloomed there
into a soft radiant field of wheat, an eternal weaving of birth and decay.
later that month she'll pass it during her cycle, milled into flour,
prepare loaves of bread and eat it.

unfortunately, the fine sister already has a girl,
and three big-assed friends who jump you and nasir
—how quickly feel goods subside into violence, dust, then ash, your ass laughing

at the end of this with nasir about catfishes—
women building whole new skins to be touched and eaten.
all this trouble began cause you had to buy a taste of feel good.
a hard lesson to learn when only the aftertaste reeks of shit.

#NOTYOURMODELSURVIVOR
Tafisha Edwards

I'm afraid to press charges
        #Irefuse to wear panties so you'll notice how firm
    this ass is because I'm always in the gym   #insomnia
my PTSD acts up at night and 50 squats will tighten just about anything

I don't make eye contact with the Salvation Army Sidewalk Santas
    #YouCantScamMe   #ImNotNewtoThis

I make prolonged eye contact with your partner(s) in Whole Foods
    which none of us can afford to shop at   But my psychiatrist said
    I needed to something something something to help my depression
#KaleAndQuinoaforAll   I skip therapy to get pedicures

search *"strap-ons for petite women"* on a stranger's borrowed phone
    and keep a rolodex of fake names for men who chat me up in airports
            (latest name: Giavanni)
    #WontPretendImSorry   #I bought myself a diamond so they'll assume
it's a wedding ring   That's right I'm one of those bitches who buys themselves diamonds
    #LizTaylorTaughtMe

I show pictures of my cousins from the 90s on Super Shuttle
                    and indiscriminately quote Bébé's Kids.
        Once I kicked a small child
    out of a bounce castle   A literal kick   I think I hate children
(this might not be the case more data is required)   I've stopped wanting to be a mother

        then broke up with Jesus   It was a me thing   #notHim

This morning I drank wine for breakfast   So   what I'm

saying is
        I have no encouraging words

                                    to give you
clearly   I fucked up somewhere
                 and I wouldn't listen to me
                         if I were you.

OUR
DIVINE CHORDS

PRINCE—ALBUM COVER

Teri Ellen Cross Davis

With the lavender dreamscape behind him
who was this god, naked astride a Pegasus?
I couldn't read the florid script, but didn't
need it to know love was feathered hair
framing a tan face, doe wide-eyes, bare
thighs gripping a white-winged horse.
This nude body was not hidden like my father's
dirty magazines, so this meant art, an invitation
drawing my gaze close, closer to determine
where divinity nestled itself between man and horse.

FINDING THE DIVINE

celeste doaks
after Prince—Album Cover

We find divinity wherever the hell we want. Music
is divinity, a nude body is divinity, even a bee is divine
despite my lack of affinity for it. What do we esteem?
A man on a winged horse? Do we dare dream of our fathers
exposed like the sexual beings they are? Patty cake patty cake
baker's man. We never grow up, we just grow older. Peek behind
the curtain and presto! We find a dove in a hopeless place,
but can hope find us kneeling, our faces turned skywards?
Crouching tiger, praying mantis. Even Atlantis fell out of favor
with the gods. Is nothing sacred? Maybe everything is holy,
an album cover, a father's lewd magazines, even the honey
is holy, glistening and sticky in our mouths.

HOUSES OF THE HOLY—LED ZEPPELIN'S ALBUM COVER

Teri Ellen Cross Davis

In this temple of bare bottoms and breast buds,
my ears follow the steps of the guitar,
each chord progression—a gospel raising
the hair on my arms. Is this what I am supposed
to feel in church? But it's Saturday and music
explodes from the speakers in the living
room. Daddy says, These white boys can rock.
He's strumming my baby sister's belly, her giddy
laughter, an improvised solo. Spinning in this
carpeted pulpit, the whites of my father's eyes
on fire, sweat pouring down his face, reverb shaking
the house. I am anointed, blessed by rock and roll.

FOR THE PURPLE ONE

celeste doaks

You mop pianos
with your chest in '94.
A quick thrust of tiny hips.
They shoot sex like a slender .22.
How can I catch your bullets?

Five feet full of funk,
jazz, rock—you shatter them all.
Play guitar like it's
a woman. Slide fingers in be-
tween her strings and make her sing.

Your song reads like Brooks.
You real cool and sing sinfully.
You Kiss worlds awake
with Sex in the Summer 'til
Little Red Corvette begins.

Purple majesty
what shall I label you now?
Sir Roger Nelson?
The artist formerly known
as an ambiguous sign?

Who cares when you live
between high heels and jumpsuits?
You who breathe tenor
and falsetto as one. You
who wear butch and belle so well.

GREAT GRANNY'S LAST NIGHT

Saida Agostini

beyond her window, she can hear the strains
men leaving the fields, singing in anticipation of another
night sweet with food and women, their faces tender
with sweat, ringed in mud
hands gripping machetes, blades slung
upwards towards a dimming sun

her pipe lays packed and unsmoked by her bed,
clean sheets huddled round her, cups of
milky tea and weeping held quiet in the next room

granny will tell me all she saw that night,
death—a great horned thing
sitting side by side with god in one small
cramped room by a huge dark river. the birds
cawing in blue ecstasy, elvis' love me tender played
on repeat until even the record player begs for relief,
the pick worn down with playing lyrics so
tired they can't help but be real

elvis in a glittery jumpsuit and heels wailing
for my darlin I love you

and when he hits that high note, pulls away
the mic, crooning love me true even
death and god dance together,
weep in each other's embrace, smiling
for an old woman losing breath as the
time bears down

she says *I jus' need him ta fuhgiv one*
las' ting made her body a confession

hands stretched out in the air towards
a white white road filled with flowers, fruit and light,
no work or babies to deliver—just liming and a
shining laughing death
ready to deliver her, a squalling wrinkly child

NOTES AND ACKNOWLEDGMENTS

The phrase "chicken wing twitch of the right arm" in Anya Creightney's poem "Leaving the House" comes directly from Simone White's poem "No Drugs, No Diseases," published by Factory House, 2010.

BLBC would like to thank deeply Mary Sherman Willis, who allowed us to stay at her lovely country home in Summer 2016 to birth some of the poems seen here in *Not Without Our Laughter*.

Saida Agostini would like to thank Delaware Poetry Review for first printing "Adventures of the Third Limb" and "What it takes to Breathe." She is abundantly thankful for her Granny, Clarice Fanny Agostini, her platonic life partner Caro Rodriguez-Fucci, and of course her mother, father and little sister, Anika.

Anya Creightney would like to thank Nick Seifert, Jen Atkinson, Sally Keith, Lannie Alexander, Cave Canem, and Vermont Studio Center.

Teri Ellen Cross Davis would like to thank Hayes Davis for being so cool and parental to our offspring, and to VCCA for time well-spent.

celeste doaks would also like to thank Karl Henzy, (who's *a pearl among pebbles*), the dope Doaks fam, and for P.D.H. May this book always provide light in times of darkness.

Tafisha Edwards would like to thank Gigantic Sequins for first printing "Husbands." She would also like to thank Allison Joseph and her Southern Illinois University Carbondale cohorts: Meghann Plunkett, Isiah Fish, Jacquelyn Zeng, Andrew Leeming, Anna Knowles, and Ira Hatfield.

Katy Richey would like to thank HEArt Online for first printing "Defendant vs. Her Remaining Eggs." She would also like to thank her mom & dad, baby daddy, friends, poetry comrades, chocolate gelato, electric blankets, thesauruses & her two freeloadin' cats.

ALL of BLBC would like to thank, in no particular order:

Writers and Words, Mason Jar Press: (Ian Anderson and Michael B. Tager), Niki Herd, Joseph Ross, D. Watkins, The Cave Canem Foundation, Sarah Browning, Split This Rock Poetry Festival, University of Baltimore, Steven Leyva, Jan Beatty, Lyrae Van-Clief Stefanon, Jane Clarke, and Bob Hicok.

THE BLACK LADIES BRUNCH COLLECTIVE IS...

SAIDA AGOSTINI

Saida Agostini is a queer Afro-Guyanese poet and social worker. A Cave Canem Fellow, her work has appeared in several publications, including pluck! The Affrilachian Journal of Arts and Culture, TORCH Literary Arts, Delaware Poetry Review and Beltway Poetry Quarterly. She is currently working on her first collection, *uprisings in a state of joy*.

ANYA CREIGHTNEY

Anya Creightney, a Cave Canem fellow, is originally from Albuquerque, New Mexico with roots in Kingston and Copenhagen. A poet, editor and coordinator, she is a Programs Specialist at the Poetry & Literature Center in the Library of Congress.

TERI ELLEN CROSS DAVIS

Teri Ellen Cross Davis is a Cave Canem fellow and is on the Advisory Committee for the biennial Split This Rock Poetry Festival. Her work can be read in many anthologies and journals. Her first collection *Haint* is published by Gival Press. She coordinates the O.B. Hardison Poetry Series for the Folger Shakespeare Library in Washington, D.C. Her website is www.poetsandparents.com.

CELESTE DOAKS

Poet and journalist celeste doaks is the author of *Cornrows and Cornfields*, (Wrecking Ball Press, UK) March 2015. Cornrows was listed as one of the Ten Best Books of 2015 by Beltway Quarterly Poetry. Her journalism has appeared in the Huffington Post, Village Voice, Time Out New York. Currently, she teaches creative writing at Morgan State University.

TAFISHA EDWARDS

Tafisha A. Edwards is the author of THE BLOODLET, winner of Phantom Books' 2016 Breitling Chapbook Prize. Her work has appeared in The Offing, PHANTOM, Bodega Magazine, The Atlas Review, The Little Patuxent Review, and other print and online publications. She is a Cave Canem Graduate fellow and an MFA candidate at Southern Illinois University Carbondale.

KATY RICHEY

Katy Richey's work has appeared in Rattle, Cincinnati Review, RHINO, The Offing and other journals. She received an honorable mention for the Cave Canem Poetry Prize and was a finalist for Tupelo Press Snowbound Chapbook Poetry Award. She is a Cave Canem fellow and hosts the Sunday Kind of Love reading series open mic at Busboys and Poets in Washington D.C.